Positi d
Afi

by Carole Davies

The secret to my success?

Belief, intention, gratitude,
love and sheer determination!

Carole Davies

To Linda
With love & best wishes
Carole xx
Christmas 2018

First published in 2012 in the United Kingdom by
Carole Davies Publishing,
www.caroledavies.com

ISBN 978-0-9572662-1-6

Carole Davies is Europe's favourite Cosmic Ordering Expert, Positive Thinking Coach and Agony Aunt. Her kind, caring and sympathetic nature has earned her immense popularity across the globe and on social networks, where she is commonly known as "Angel Lady Carole"

You are a creative, unique and divine being, capable of manifesting anything and everything your heart desires.

By becoming the person you truly want to be, success shall be yours.

Allow intent to be your
personal assistant, it can fill
your hopes, dreams and
ambitions and action them
at your will.

Your unlimited enthusiasm
will be your catalyst, allowing
you to succeed in
everything you do.

By being ruled by the
heart and not the head,
you shall truly find
your soul.

Every successful
achievement began with
YOU making that all
important choice.

Learn to forgive those who may have hurt you. The pain was your stepping stone towards greater things.

Focus on your life being magnificent and it WILL BE magnificent.

THINK OF YOUR LIFE
STRETCHING OUT
AHEAD OF YOU AND
LOOK FORWARD TO
A FUTURE OF
FREEDOM, PEACE
AND SPACE,
SURROUNDED BY A
UNIVERSE OF LOVE.

Follow the light and love within
your soul, for light is what we are
and love is what we give.

Get back in the driver's seat and
take control of your life, there is so
much to see and do, the real
beauty is in the journey.

Take a step back and look at the
whole picture then focus on what
you really want - it's yours for the
taking.

Understanding Cosmic Ordering is
easy - we bring to us what we
think about. Happy thoughts
create happy lives, unhappy
thoughts can generate their equal.

WHEN YOU
LOVE AND ACCEPT
YOURSELF YOU
CANNOT FAIL
TO BE
AMAZING

STOP LIVING FOR
OTHER PEOPLE AND
THEIR CHOICES, LEARN
TO VALUE YOURSELF
AND WHAT YOU
STAND FOR –
BE BOLD – BE YOU

ALWAYS GIVE THANKS
FOR WHAT YOU ALREADY
HAVE AND WHAT YOU
ARE ABOUT TO HAVE,
ALLOW AN ATTITUDE OF
GRATITUDE TO BE YOUR
CATALYST IN
MANIFESTING YOUR
HOPES AND DREAMS.

Always follow your heart,
listen to your inner
thoughts, trust yourself. Feel
the love inside you and let it
flow outwards.

Knowing that you are a
beacon of light for others
creates happiness and joy.

Who cares about job titles,
the person that you are is far
more important than the job
that you do.

Don't give up on your
dreams no matter what is
thrown at you, your desire
and intention to change
things will remove all
obstacles.

I CHOOSE TO LOVE MYSELF AND NOURISH MY BODY, MIND AND SOUL WITH HEALTH, WEALTH AND HAPPINESS

I AM CREATIVE,

CARING,

LOVING AND

UNIQUE

When you associate
situations with negative
feelings you will attract
negativity.
By switching your mindset
to positive mode, your whole
perspective will change for
the better.

It doesn't take much to

create a happy life.

The answer is within us

and the way

we choose to think.

Think outside the box and you will discover that you can achieve that which in the past you had only dared to dream.

Share with that someone
special today how much they
mean to you. They deserve
to be reminded once
in a while.

Take the time to reflect on life's opportunities and release all negative thoughts and feelings.

Those who **believe** in themselves will **go far,** **further** than they ever imagined **possible.**

To live a life of **abundance** wealth alone is not enough. One needs **love**, laughter, **freedom** and a sprinkling of **sunshine**.

Yesterday, today,
tomorrow and beyond are a
product of your thoughts
and imagination.

What you choose to do on a
daily basis formulates
your future.

Experiences from the past
are part and parcel of
your spiritual growth,
enabling you to evolve
and progress.

Open the windows of your
mind, let the light shine in
to overcome any
shadows of darkness.

DON'T CLOSE YOUR

EYES TO

POSSIBILITIES,

THEY ARE

AND ALWAYS

WILL BE THERE.

FORGIVING YOURSELF
WILL ENABLE YOU TO
BLOSSOM AND MOVE
FORWARD, LEAVING
THE PAST BEHIND AND
OPENING THE WINDOW
TO NEW BEGINNINGS.

KEEP GOING ...

DON'T EVER GIVE UP.

THERE IS

ALWAYS HOPE

ALWAYS HOPE

ALWAYS HOPE

ALWAYS HOPE

Allow intuition to
point you in the
right direction and
let your vision
take you there.

Small beginnings
can lead to
outstanding
endings.

A single thought
can lead to many

positive outcomes.

Accept your fears
and worries but
look at them as
figments of your
imagination.

Each day you have a choice of

which path to take. You can

take the path of doubt

and fear or the path

of confidence

and positivity.

No-one can hurt

you unless you

allow them to.

Creativity is not reserved for

artists. Each of us is able

to paint new colours

and bring fresh

perspectives

into our lives.

Be the catalyst in

your own life and

you will never

look back.

USE YOUR
IMAGINATION
TO CREATE
YOUR REALITY

IT WORKS

OPEN UP YOUR
HEART AND
BREATHE.
ONCE YOUR
HEART IS OPEN
TO OTHERS
YOU BEGIN TO
LIVE

WHEN I FIND
MYSELF FEELING
NEGATIVE, I SIMPLY
RECALIBRATE,
INTRODUCING
POSITIVE AND
LOVING THOUGHTS,
BRINGING ME THE
GIFT OF HAPPINESS,
PEACE AND JOY

AS I LOOK AROUND
ME TODAY I SHALL
FIND SOMETHING
BEAUTIFUL AND
POSITIVE IN
EVERTHING I SEE AND
EVERYONE I MEET

If you lose hold of your identity, don't worry. This is the perfect time to visualise a new and amazing you.

Problems only exist
in our own mind.
You will always find
a solution, you are
destined to.

Look through the
windows of your
mind and see your
thoughts, feelings
and beliefs waiting to
be actioned.

Don't tumble over
what's ahead
simply because
you keep looking
back.

Don't turn a misfortune into

a crisis, see it as an

opportunity for adventure

and new beginnings.

Our thoughts will weave life's

tapestry and make us who we

are meant to be.

By making small steps in the right direction your future will not only be defined but realised.

Allow praise to change your gaze, radiating beauty from your heart.

With patience and by
practising meditation
you can achieve the
perfect mindset
to reach your
goals.

By making your wish now,
you are bringing its
realisation even
closer.

The smallest of gifts
can mean so much,
especially if it is
given with
love.

Miracles do exist,
with a little
help from
you.

Live your life in

grace and serenity,

be grateful for

what you have and

look forward to

future gifts and

opportunities.

Take a chance and
break away from old
beliefs and habits.
Open your mind
and allow loving
energy and optimism
to take control of
your life.

There are no limits
on our dreams.
The more we dream
the more possibilities
and opportunities
we discover.

THE UNIVERSE IS FULL
OF AMAZING
MAGICAL MYSTERIES·
IT'S UP TO US
TO DISCOVER THEM·

LET THE DRAMA CEASE
AND LET IN THE PEACE,
IT'S WAITING
IN THE WINGS·

Do what you love
with great joy and
commitment
and success will
follow.

Beauty is all
around us,
everywhere we go,
but we have to
open our eyes
to see it.

MAKE your DREAM
your INTENTION.
FOCUS ON IT,
BELIEVE IN IT, MAKE IT
YOUR REALITY.

MAKE EACH DAY
YOUR OWN SPECIAL
MIRACLE BY GIVING,
CARING AND SHARING.
YOU WILL SURELY
REAP THE REWARDS.

NEVER be afraid of
making changes or
CREATING success
in your LIFE.

DONT worry about
all your
YESTERDAYS, instead
FOCUS on your
BRIGHT
and BEAUTIFUL
tomorrows.

No one can stop you
achieving your goals
and ambitions providing
that you stay in the
correct mode of thinking.
Positive is as positive does.

Sometimes the most
difficult experiences can
be the most satisfying and
rewarding of all.

Each and every one of
us are on this life's path
together, no one is
more important than
anyone else.
We all have a valuable
contribution to make.

Dont occupy your mind
by worrying about
what's right for others,
instead focus on what's
right for yourself.

TODAY I CHOOSE
TO CONNECT
WITH MY HIGHER
SELF AND FIND MY
INNER HARMONY
AND PEACE

BY LETTING GO OF

GRUDGES AND

GRIEVENCES I AM

ABLE TO LIVE MY

LIFE IN FREEDOM

AND LOVE

Teach yourself to accept compliments. They are genuine truths that tell you how amazing you really are.

Now is the time

to open up to the

abundance that is

all around you,

for no one is more

deserving than

you.

Broaden your mind and
open up your heart,
allowing love in and all
grudges and grievances
of the past and present
to fall away.

By allowing others to be
who they want to be,
you open up
opportunities for
yourself, allowing you
to be who you want to
be too.

Be brave enough to leave your comfort zone, you won't regret it.

Hold close that
which is dear to your
heart and with
an angel's breath,
let the rest go.

ONCE GRATITUDE
BECOMES PART OF
YOUR DAILY LIVING,
ABUNDANCE WON'T
BE FAR BEHIND.

NO ONE HAS TO BE
BIG TO BECOME
GREAT, WE ARE ALL
WORTHY.

THE TYPE OF
THOUGHTS THAT
YOU HAVE,
MANIFESTS THE
QUALITY OF LIFE
THAT YOU LEAD.

BELIEVE IN
MIRACLES AND THEY
WILL BE YOURS.

SOMETIMES WE NEED TO
THINK LIKE A CHILD,
FORGET OUR
RESPONSIBILITIES FOR A
WHILE AND PLAY. WE TOO
CAN WONDER AT NATURE,
DAYDREAM AND SEE THE
JOY IN SIMPLE THINGS. WE
NEED TO LEARN TO LET GO.
IT'S AT THESE TIMES THAT
WE REALISE THAT OUR
WILDEST FANTASIES CAN
BECOME REALITY.

Achieve your **destiny** by
making those much
needed **choices**, you are
not just the choice
maker but the master of
dreams.

Think you will do it,
and you WILL
do it.

Why do we underestimate
the power of our
thoughts, feelings
and beliefs?
They are the creators of
who we are and who
we shall be.

New beginnings are
only hard if you
want them
to be.

There is still time to turn an
enemy into a friend. By
letting go of grievances and
knocking down the walls
that have been built between
you, you're in a perfect
position to let love in and
friendship begin.

We have to change in order
to grow. If we don't grow
we can't live life to the full.

It takes strength and
courage to become who you
want to be. By practising
determination, intent and
gratitude, you will be.

Age is and always will be
whatever you determine it
to be.

You have the power
and strength to bring
down all the
obstacles that stand
in your way.

Imagination changed
my whole life and it
can change yours
too.

Give yourself a positive push in the right direction and enjoy the endless opportunities that await you.

Always live in love, it's the best way to be and the best expression you can give.

OPEN UP THE GATES OF

OPPORTUNITY, FOCUS ON

WHAT YOU WANT AND WHERE

YOU WISH TO GO, REALITY AND

A NEW WAY OF LIFE AWAITS

YOU

YOUR OWN IMAGINATION IS

THE ONLY BLOCK TO

FULFILLING YOUR HOPES AND

DREAMS

DONT THINK BACK, THINK

FORWARD – IT'S THE ONLY WAY

TO GO

Be the spark to the flame, ignite passion into to your life and watch your dreams and ambitions come alive.

Reading
inspirational quotes
and affirmations
will not only
encourage you to
think positively, it
will allow
you to see more
clearly too, enabling
you to create a
pathway to a bright,
happy and
successful future.

I AM AWARE OF
THE LOVE THAT
FLOWS
THROUGH ME
AND AROUND
ME

TODAY I TAP INTO
WHAT COMES
STRAIGHT FROM
MY HEART -
LOVE, COMPASSION
AND
UNDERSTANDING

When you fall at that first hurdle, pick yourself up and try even harder. The finishing line is still within your reach.

Open yourself up to
accepting your hopes,
dreams and desires -
they are yours for the
taking.

BE CAREFUL WHAT
YOU SAY AND DO
BECAUSE THE PERSON
WHO WILL HAVE TO
LIVE WITH THE
CONSEQUENCES IS YOU.

EACH OF US ARE MORE
COURAGEOUS THAN
WE THINK, LET FEAR
DISAPPEAR AND THE
ROAD TO VICTORY
WILL APPEAR.

LIFE IS A WONDERFUL
AND ONGOING
DISCOVERY. TAKE THE
TIME TO MAKE USE OF
AND ENJOY ALL THE
OPPORTUNITIES IT
BESTOWS UPON YOU.

LOSS OF ENTHUSIASM
CAN QUASH YOUR
CHANCE OF SUCCESS.

Failure is not in my
vocabulary, it is simply
another chance to start
over again.

Instead of going with the
flow, focus on letting go.
Once you get your
thoughts in gear, the way
ahead will be crystal
clear.

Reinvention is always a possibility and it is available to everyone, choose your path and walk the walk.

Being defeatist is only a permanent condition if you allow it to be.

THE UNIVERSE
PROVIDES US WITH
THIS BEAUTIFUL
ESSENCE OF LIFE,
BY SPREADING ITS
INFINITIVE LOVE
DAY IN AND DAY
OUT.

REFUSE TO
ACCEPT ANYTHING
BUT THE BEST AND
YOU WILL NOT
HAVE TO SETTLE
FOR ANYTHING
LESS.

PROBLEM,...
WHAT PROBLEM?
CHANGE YOUR
WAY OF THINKING
AND THE PROBLEM
WILL BE SOLVED.

Practice
forgiveness
and make it a
habit, it
opens up a
multitude of
opportunities.

Allow things
that have
happened in the
past to be a
learning curve,
not something
to shun or run
from, but
something to
learn from.

Value and treasure
yourself and others will
too.

Stop devaluing yourself,
you are a one off, divine
and unique human being.
Focus on your qualities,
for you have many.

Trust the fact that you
will meet the right
people at the right time.
It is all part of the divine
plan, your life's path.

Your path to a bright and
happy new future begins
from the moment you
wake.

Sticking to one's opinion takes a lot of courage. Have that courage to be who you really are and express how you really feel.

Your every thought is an opportunity to bring new beginnings into your life.

By thinking, acting and living with a positive outlook you will bring into your life positive experiences.

Never give in or give up.
Your dedication and
motivation to make the
changes you desire comes
from within. You are the
creator of your own future.

By making the changes
you want to see, you can
live your life and be totally
free.

Don't allow the nostalgic chapters of your past to prevent you trom turning a crisp new page.

Patience, love and understanding. Practice these three and they will be returned to you.

Apart from love
being the most
powerful force in
our lives, giving and
forgiving can send
out the most positive
vibes. Join the three
and you shall see,
loving, giving and
forgiving is the only
way to be.

~⊶⊙⊷~

By having kind
positive thoughts
and feelings
towards ourselves
we create a feel
good factor and
this in return brings
to us more of the
same.

~⊶⊙⊷~

IT IS MY GOAL
TO MAKE A
DIFFERENCE,
NOT ONLY IN
MY LIFE BUT IN
THE LIVES OF
OTHERS

NEW BEGINNINGS
WAIT FOR ME.
MY GIFT OF
FREE WILL
SETS ME FREE

We can change
our world by
changing
ourselves. The
actions we choose
and choices we
make will
facilitate our
transformation.

Allow a glimmer
of positivity to
shine through in
everything you
do and life will
be good to you.

NOW IS THE TIME TO LET

GO OF ALL NEGATIVE

THOUGHTS AND FEELINGS,

BY RADIATING LOVE AND

HAVING A POSITIVE

OUTLOOK YOU WILL BE

CAPABLE OF DOING

ANYTHING YOU DESIRE.

In Spite of your fears,

choose to Be the

unstoppable force in

your life. You can

change your mindset

with Just A Single

thought, By trusting

your instinct And

listening to your heart

THE DOORS TO
YOUR FUTURE ARE
ALWAYS OPEN,
AN ABUNDANCE OF
OPPORTUNITIES
AWAITS YOU ON
THE OTHER SIDE.

Live life to the full and by
transforming your limiting
beliefs, practising gratitude and
believing in yourself, the
universe will be inspired to
bring your hopes and dreams to
reality.

Refrain from being competitive
for it is fear based, serves no
purpose in our lives and simply
magnifies the fact that we are
afraid of others having more.
Instead live in love.

Love is warm, comforting and
creative, it can be shared with
another without the fear of
inequality.

There comes a time in your life when you need to let go of negativity and the people and situations that create it. Surround yourself with love, people who make you smile and those who encourage you to focus on the positive and good things in life.

Keep in your life

those who inspire

you and allow

you to be

yourself.

Decide what

success means for

you and with great

passion, take

action.

BEING SUCCESSFUL
IN LIFE ISN'T ONLY
ABOUT YOU, IT'S ALSO
ABOUT OTHERS AND
HOW YOU CAN BE
THEIR CATALYST OF
INSPIRATION TO
ENABLE THEM TO
BECOME SUCCESSFUL
TOO.

WHEN YOU FOCUS
ON YOUR GOALS,
YOU ARE AT YOUR
STRONGEST AND
MOST POWERFUL.

CELEBRATE LIFE AND
LIVE, VISUALISE
YOUR GOALS AND
AMBITIONS AND BY
LIVING IN LOVE, ALL
THE GIFTS YOU SEEK
WILL BE YOURS.

Focus on having a bright and beautiful tomorrow and it will come to pass.

Listen to the loving voice of the universe. It is always there to cheer you on.

As you become older,
look on your age in a
positive light. Learn
from the good times
and move on from
negative
experiences.

Let the beams of love
shine through and all
good things will
come to you.

THERE IS ONLY ONE
PERSON WHO DOES THE
THINKING INSIDE YOUR
HEAD. THAT ONE PERSON
IS YOU. WHERE YOUR
THOUGHTS AND FEELINGS
HAVE BEEN, YOU WILL GO.
YOU ARE THE DECISION
MAKER

BE MORE SUPPORTIVE
AND LESS REACTIVE. THIS
CLEARS THE PATH
TOWARDS HAVING MORE
MEANINGFUL
RELATIONSHIPS BASED
ON LOVE AND
UNDERSTANDING

FORGIVING
YOURSELF WILL
ENABLE YOU TO
BLOSSOM AND
MOVE FORWARD,
LEAVING PAST
EVENTS BEHIND
AND THE
WINDOW OPEN
TO NEW
BEGINNINGS.

Sometimes you
have to push
the reset
button and
start over.
Don't let your
history stop
your destiny.

Be generous
and loving to
the universe
and the
universe will
be generous
and loving to
you too.

I am a vessel
of peace,
tranquility
and love. My
soul lies deep
within the
heart of me
transcending
all that I am
and all I that
ever will be.

You are the
master builder of
your life, every
positive choice
and decision you
make creates a
firm foundation to
build upon.

Love and believe
in yourself,
focus on your
inner beauty
and self-esteem.
Your world will
feel renewed.

You are the
captain of your
ship, cast your
net with certainty
and commitment
and you shall
reap the rewards.

Feel and see the
beauty of the
universe working
each and every
moment in your
favour, bringing to
you your hearts
desires.

Doing a good deed
inspires others and
inspires ourselves
too.

When you have
happiness,
forgiveness comes
easy.

I ACCEPT

RESPONSIBILITY

FOR BOTH MY

ACTIONS AND MY

REACTIONS AND I

CHOOSE TO LIVE

IN PEACE, LOVE

AND LIGHT

I HAVE THE KEY

TO THE DOOR,

FEAR SHALL

OVERCOME ME

NO MORE

Don't allow tunnel vision to control your desires. Open up your heart and mind to fulfill your aspirations.

Choose happiness

every time and your

life will become

simply divine.

DON'T BE AFRAID TO SPREAD THOSE BEAUTIFUL WINGS, IT'S YOUR TURN TO FLY.

CIRCUMSTANCES
ARE NEVER SO
WRONG THAT
THEY CAN'T EVER
BE RIGHT

NEVER GIVE UP ON
YOURSELF, A
SOLUTION IS JUST A
THOUGHT AWAY,
THEN SUCCESS WILL
BE YOURS

There are many people in this world, but in the end, to make that all important life changing decision, it comes down to only one ...

... YOU!!!

May love and

light be with you

always,

Carole Davies

About Cosmic Ordering and Positive Thinking

With dedication and a positive attitude you can achieve all the things you've only dreamed about through Cosmic Ordering and Positive Thinking.

Cosmic ordering and the cosmos, the law of attraction and the universe, the secret, positive thinking … It really doesn't matter what name, label, or tag you choose, all are one and the same. They are not some sort of craze or new invention. Manifesting what you want has been going on for thousands of years. As the Roman Emperor Marcus Aurelius, AD 121-180, said

"The happiness of your life depends on the quality of your thoughts"

I was recently speaking to a friend who had been a Project Manager for a large IT consulting firm in the UK and as I started to tell him about the processes involved in Cosmic Ordering he smiled and looked extremely smug. He said these weren't Cosmic Ordering techniques but that they were project management techniques that he'd been using for years. This had pretty much convinced him that this "new fangled thing called Cosmic Ordering" was "all nonsense."

I agreed that the techniques had a cross over but then why shouldn't they? It's about taking specific actions to achieve a specific goal after all.

I asked my friend if when using his techniques he'd ever failed at a project. He admitted he had, but only because some element of the "Plan Of Action" had been overlooked or changed without regard to the outcome. He told me about one project where they had halved the number of people working on the team but kept the deadlines. The equivalent for your Cosmic Order would be to doubt yourself or the Universe and still expect to receive your order.

Cosmic Ordering is not only about thinking positive thoughts but also believing in those thoughts. It's about placing your order, believing that you deserve to achieve your life's ambition and being grateful.

Gratitude is one of the most important elements of Cosmic Ordering and Positive Thinking, but also the most overlooked.

We need to give thanks to the Universe for our orders, this in turn opens us up to receive more.

The improvements in your life that will come from believing in yourself will change you and your life more than any other single thing you do even without all the additional benefits that will come your way from Cosmic Ordering and Positive Thinking.

"The things that we feel and think about, we bring about"

A little about me

I have always been a spiritual being. Originally I thought my role would be that of a psychic medium following my first experience of survival after death at just eighteen. Life, however, took me towards a more caring role as a nurse for a well know cancer care organisation. As my life progressed I found myself being drawn more and more to the spiritual side, including experiences of visualisation, synchronicity, and angelic communication. In turn I soon became interested in the universe and often found myself sitting up until the early hours researching the subject, giving in only when my eyes refused to see any longer. I learned that Positive Thinking and Cosmic Ordering are real and that by simply shifting your thought patterns and beliefs you can achieve your hopes and dreams!

My next book

I am really excited about my new book. It gives a little more insight into how, when and where the first angels were discovered and how, throughout the centuries, they have helped and guided both the human and animal species from the beginning of creation to the present day.

It also explains the who's who in the Hierarchy of Angels, the roles that they play and how little most of us know about these truly amazing celestial beings.

Angels appear in different ways to different people. All of this and much more will be revealed, including astounding real life accounts shared with me by many wonderful people from all corners of the world.

For more information about this book and my other up and coming projects go to:

www.caroledavies.com

NOTES

NOTES

NOTES

NOTES

NOTES

NOTES